WHY Is the snapdragon called so ?

Om KIDZ
An imprint of Om Books International

Contents

Why are plants called the 'lungs of the Earth'?

Because they give us fresh air! Trees are often called the 'lungs of the Earth' because they take in carbon dioxide from the air and give out oxygen. Oxygen is vital for the existence of humans and animals. If there were no plants there would be an increase in the level of carbon dioxide in the air, which would lead to global warming and climate change as well.

Pocket fact

130 million years ago!
Plants did not bear flowers when they first appeared on Earth. Flowering plants and flowers appeared around 130 million years ago.

Find out

Name three trees that provide us wood.

Why can't we live without plants?

They are very important for our survival! Humans have three basic necessities: oxygen, water and food. Plants produce oxygen, which is very essential for our existence. Plants also form the basis of our entire food chain. In addition to this, plants also provide us with wood, herbs, spices, paper, cotton and many other things.

Why are plants green and not black in colour?

Because they reflect green light! Objects appear to be of a certain colour because they absorb some wavelengths of light and reflect others. For example, a black shirt appears black because it absorbs all the wavelengths of light and doesn't reflect any light. Plants are largely filled with green pigments called chlorophyll that absorb sunlight and reflect green light. Plants would be black in colour if chlorophyll absorbed all the light and reflected none.

Pocket fact

Good weeds!

Weeds may not always be harmful. Some weeds like the stinging nettles are full of vitamin C and are often used in herbal medicines as they are beneficial for health.

Try this!

Take a potted plant and cover one of its leaves with black paper. Keep it on the window sill. Remove the paper after 2-3 days. What do you observe?

Why are weeds not good for other plants?

Because they hamper the growth of other plants! Weeds are unwanted plants that grow on their own near crops or other plants. They are not good for other plants because they compete with them for water, light and nutrients. Many weeds also act as hosts to pests and thus harm the other plants by spreading diseases.

Why are root hairs thin?

So that they can absorb water and nutrients from the soil! The roots of a plant not only keep the plant fixed in the soil but they also have tiny, thin root hairs with a large surface area, which help them absorb water and nutrients from the soil.

Try this!

Take a celery stalk and put it in blue coloured water. Observe the plant after 4–5 days. Why did the stalk change its colour?

Pocket fact

We need help!
There are certain roots that do not work at their best unless they have help from fungi. The symbiosis between roots and fungus is known as mycorrhiza.

Why do roots wear caps?

To protect themselves! The root cap is a section of tissue at the tip of a plant root. It covers the sensitive root and protects the growing tip in plants. It also secretes a fluid to ease the movement of the root through soil, thus enabling its downward growth.

Why do mangroves have breathing roots?

Because they get little oxygen! Mangrove trees are found around tropical coasts all over the world. Although they are land plants, they grow in saltwater with their roots buried in thick soil that contains little oxygen. In order to breathe, the roots send up spikes that rise into the air above the level of the mud. These spikes exchange oxygen and expel carbon dioxide into the air, and help the tree breathe.

Find out

What are tendrils?

Pocket fact

That's strange!

Not all climbers grow in the same way! The Climbing Fetterbush doesn't use clinging roots, tendrils or thorns. Its stem goes into a crack in the bark of fibrous-barked trees and flattens. It then grows up the tree from underneath the outer bark.

Why do some roots climb and cling?

They help the weak plants climb! Some plants such as the Irish ivy have weak stems and thus cannot stand upright. These plants have a cluster of short, stout roots that cling to surfaces. Such roots are modified roots that come out of the nodes and help the plant to climb up around a support.

Why do some trees lose their leaves?

To prevent water loss! Trees lose a lot of water from their leaves due to evaporation. When winter approaches, trees stop the production of the growth hormone and form a seal over the spots where leaves are attached to them. Then, water and nutrients stop flowing from the tree to the leaves, thus preventing water loss from the tree. Over time, the leaves gradually lose their moisture. Eventually they dry up and fall off the tree.

Find out

Which part of the leaf helps in the exchange of gases?

Pocket fact

No salt please!

Moss can grow anywhere on Earth except in saltwater.

Why do mosses grow in moist areas?

Because they don't have roots, leaves or stems! Moss is a flowerless plant that grows in clumps. They don't have roots but have thin root-like parts called rhizoids that help to fix the plant in the soil. Since they don't have roots and stems to transport water, mosses dry out very quickly, so they are usually found in moist habitats.

Why do flowers disappear from a plant?

Because they turn into fruits! Flowers are the parts of a plant that turn into fruits after pollination. During pollination, the pollen moves from the anthers to the stigma. When the pollen lands on the stigma, a pollen tube develops and fertilizes the ovary at the base of the flower. After fertilization the flower eventually turns into a fruit and the ovules form the seeds.

Find out

Can you name three flowers that bloom at night?

Pocket fact

Flowery desserts!
Flowers are not only used for ornamental purposes but also for decorating food items. Dahlias are used to decorate cakes, tarts, pastries, salads and for garnishing desserts.

Why do moon flowers bloom only at night?

Because they are adapted to pollination by moths! Moon flowers are plants with large, round, white flowers that open in the evening and wither by morning. They bloom only at night because they are pollinated by moths and most moths are active only during the night. Their large size and white colour make them more noticeable to the moths in the moonlight.

Why do dandelion seeds fly?

So that they can get a suitable place to grow! Plant seeds are dispersed to different places so that they don't grow very close to the parent plant. Seeds of plants like dandelions and cottonwood are light and have feathery bristles. The wind carries them to far-off places. If these seeds land in a suitable place, they begin to grow.

Pocket fact

So many uses!
All the parts of a dandelion plant are edible. Its leaves are a rich source of Vitamin K and its flowers can be used to make wine. Its roots can be used to make a brewed drink that tastes a bit like coffee!

Find out

Can seeds sprout without soil?

Why don't seeds grow in my stomach when I swallow them?

Because it is not a suitable place for seeds to grow! Seeds will grow only when they are planted in places where they can get the nutrients essential for their growth. Your stomach is full of acidic digestive juices and doesn't have the nutrients that a seed needs for its growth. Thus, it is not a hospitable place for plants to grow!

Why do potatoes grow under the ground?

Because the potato plant has a modified stem! Some plants have bulbs or tubers like onions that help them in storing food. A potato is actually a tuber or a swollen stem— a fleshy growth that is attached to the roots underground. It stores extra water and nutrients for the plant's future use.

Pocket fact

Smelly without rotting!

Some fruits smell bad while they are still on the plant. The Durian, also known as `the king of fruits', is by far the smelliest fruit in the world.

Find out

Can potatoes grow in space?

Why don't fruits rot on plants?

Because they are not exposed to microorganisms! When fruits are attached to their parent plant, they are nourished and protected by the plant. When a fruit detaches from the plant, it is exposed to air. Then microorganisms attack the fruit and begin their work of breaking it down for their own uses. They also use the water within the fruit and eventually destroy the fruit.

Why doesn't a cactus need water?

Because it has certain abilities that allow it to conserve water! A cactus has an extensive, but shallow, root system that allows it to soak up water. It has specialized stems that help it store water for long durations. Cactus has leaves that are modified into thorns. This reduces water loss and also prevents the cactus from being eaten up by animals. For example, a fully-grown Saguaro Cactus can soak up and store up to 200 gallons of water during a good downpour! Many desert travellers have learned that, in case of an emergency, a cactus can be opened to find life-saving fluids.

Pocket fact

Cactus is my home!
The Gila woodpecker nests inside the stem of the Saguaro Cactus where the temperature may be up to 30°C (86°F), which is cooler than the temperature outside.

Try this!

Explore the different kinds of cacti around the world. Which cacti are your favourites?

Why is the cactus prickly?

Because its leaves have been turned into thorns! A cactus is a plant that usually grows in the desert or where the soil is dry and rocky. It doesn't have leaves like other plants do. A cactus has spines or thorns that are actually highly-modified leaves. The spines help to reduce water loss from the cactus and also protect it from animals.

Why is the four o'clock plant named so?

Because it blooms late in the afternoon! The four o'clock plant, also known as `beauty-of-the-night' is an ornamental plant that grows in tropical America. It is called four o'clock because the petals of these flowers open late in the afternoon and close by morning. The flowers vary in colour from white and yellow to shades of pink and red. They are sometimes streaked and mottled.

Pocket fact

The tallest sunflower!

The tallest sunflower recorded by The Guinness World Records measures 9.17 m. It was grown by Hans-Peter Schiffer in Karst, Nordrhein Westfalen, Germany.

Find out

How is the four o'clock plant useful to us?

Why do sunflowers chase the sun?

So that they can maximise photosynthesis! The fascinating phenomenon of flowers following the Sun across the sky is called heliotropism. This phenomenon is seen in sunflowers when they are still young flower heads. When the flowers face the Sun it maximises the amount of direct solar radiation received. This increases the rate of photosynthesis and enhances growth.

Why do some plants eat insects?

Because they can't make their own food! We know that plants carry out photosynthesis and produce their own food. But there are some plants that do not have chlorophyll and cannot produce their own food. Hence they feed on insects and tiny creatures to survive. The Pitcher Plant and Venus Flytrap are examples of such plants.

Find out

Plants don't have a nervous system. So, how do they defend themselves from danger?

Pocket fact

Largest carnivore!
The largest carnivorous plant is Borneo's Nepenthes rajah. It has a big pitcher that can hold more than half a gallon of fluid.

Why don't plants sleep?

Because they don't have a nervous system! Sleep is a condition that is essential in humans and animals. It occurs in living beings that have a nervous system. Plants don't have a nervous system so they don't sleep. But plants do exhibit day-night cycles. They carry out photosynthesis during the day. At night, they open their stoma to take in oxygen, and deliver glucose throughout the plant. Some plants also close their flowers when the sun sets.

Why are forget-me-not flowers called so?

The name comes from a Greek word! Forget-me-not plants are plants of the Myosotis genus. This flower gets its name from the Greek word Vergissmeinnicht. This unusual Greek name means mouse's ear, which is a description of the shape of the flower's small petals.

Find out

How did the touch-me-not plant get its name?

Pocket fact

Water it enough!
A money plant requires an adequate amount of water in its initial days. So ensure that you water it enough but see that it is not soaked in water!

Why is the money plant named so?

Because its flowers have silver seedpods! Lunaria annua, also known as the money plant, or silver dollar plant, has reddish purple or white flowers that are borne in summer. In the United States, Lunaria is commonly known as `silver dollars', `Chinese money, or `Chinese coins' because its silver quarter shaped seedpods have the appearance of silvery coins.

Why is the snapdragon called so?

Because it resembles a dragon! Snapdragon is a plant that grows in western North America. The flowers are tubular and usually have a large closed, lip-like mouth. They resemble the face of a dragon and open and close their mouth when laterally squeezed.

Find out

What are the different colours of snapdragons?

Pocket fact

No more water!
Euphorbia plants should not be overwatered. Excessive water leads to the rotting of the plant.

Why is the Euphorbia obesa called the `baseball plant'?

Because it looks like a ball! Euphorbia obesa is a plant that grows in South Africa. It is commonly known as the `baseball plant' due to its ball-like shape. It is thornless with a diameter of 6–15 centimetres. It contains water reservoirs for periods of drought.

Index